REBUILD

REBUILD

Brick by Brick 7 Steps to Rebuilding a Better You

CURTIS RICE

Rev. date: 01/05/2017

To order additional copies of this book, contact:
Xlibris
1-888-795-4274
www.Xlibris.com
Orders@Xlibris.com

744889

Contents

DEDICATION

This book is dedicated to the late Chadwick Gentry (a.k.a. Boo Boo) and Melissa Edwards, two of the strongest people I know. It is through your inspiration to fight through your struggles that I have found the willpower to write this book.

Introduction

As I was sitting in my high school class in September of 2001, daydreaming while I should have been paying attention, the teacher stopped dead in midsentence to turn on the television. To our surprise, we watched as Fox News replayed a day that changed America. By now you probably know what day I am talking about: 9/11.

As I watched the debris fly around in the sky from my desk, I wondered how the families of the victims were going to rebuild. How was America as a whole going to rebuild?

After a year had passed, the time that it took to clean up the dead bodies and debris from the attack, speculations had leaked out that President George W. Bush pledged to rebuild the Trade Center.

The dedication of the Trade Center has been done and it is open for business and tourism. But even though America has moved forward, how can you possibly rebuild from a situation like that? Thousands of lives were lost in one day. Thousands of individuals were directly impacted from the attack. Children will have to go through their lives without a father or mother. People in the Trade Center were at the peaks of their careers.

No matter how many years have passed, the inner struggle will still be there. The golden question will still exist for the families that were directly impacted by such a terrible attack: How can we rebuild?

Let's fast forward. As I sit on my couch mustering up enough energy to write this paragraph, I am watching CNN discuss the mass shootings that have shattered several lives over the past decade.

It breaks my heart to hear this innocent mother say that her son would have been going into the fourth grade but that is not possible now because of a culprit. Another mother is sharing how her daughter was murdered in a movie theater. But what amazes me from listening is that both mothers are determined to rebuild, like President George W. Bush.

Have you ever faced a terrible situation that left you wondering, "How am I going to rebound from this?" If we are all honest, we all have asked that question once or twice in our lives. We are all rebuilding, whether you realize it or not. Think about it:

Your child just went off to college. It is time to rebuild.

You experienced a divorce. It is time to rebuild.

You lost a job. It is time to rebuild.

You moved to a new community. It is time to rebuild.

You lost a loved one. It is time to rebuild.

Your best friend walked out of your life. It is time to rebuild.

You just purchased a new home. It is time to rebuild.

I believe you get my point. Rebuilding is a phase in life we all will experience. Now, rebuilding your life is an option. You have to choose to rebuild from a divorce. You have to choose to rebuild from bankruptcy. You have to choose to rebuild from a lost job. You have to choose to rebuild from abuse. President George W. Bush had to choose to begin the process of rebuilding the World Trade Center. The two mothers who lost their children from a mass shooting had to choose to rebuild.

After I lost my mom at the age of ten, I had to learn how to go through life without her. After I lost my dad at the age of seventeen, I had to learn how to go through life without him. After I dropped out of high school, I had to learn how to rebuild. After the death of my younger brother, I had to learn how to go through life without him (I will share more about those experiences later in the book).

Let me pause and make a statement: Rebuilding is not easy. The process is treacherous and strenuous. But if you hang in there, you will experience a new life you never dreamed of having. You will experience a new peace, joy, and laughter.

The divorce is not the end.

The bad doctor's report is not the end.

The lost job is not the end.

The failed exam is not the end.

The "You are not accepted" is not the end.

The "You are not approved" is not the end.

If you want to rebuild, the good news is that you can do it!

The Story Behind the Book

I experienced a devastating situation a couple of years ago that brought me to my knees and sucked every ounce of faith I had out of me.

I received a phone call that a car had fallen on top of my brother. What? What was I going to do? How could I make it through this? Honestly, it probably was the first time in my life that I faced depression head-on. There were some days when I did not desire to get up and be productive. There were some days when I wanted to put my phone on silent and ignore the whole world. I was one thought from dropping out of college and one pen stroke from resigning from everything I was involved in.

My brother was in a nursing home for the next four years of his life. After every nursing home visit, I struggled with life. I could not understand why a young man in his midtwenties would have to live in a nursing home.

When the accident happened, it brought up old hurts that I was holding in, like the deaths of my parents. Simultaneously, I was dealing with a bad doctors' report about my son. To make matters worse, I learned that my brother would never walk again. I lost it. Needless to say, I became depressed. Yes, I believe in God. Yes, I pray. But I still fell into depression. I needed help. I needed answers.

Instead of blaming God for the situation, I did what I thought was best: opened the Bible for answers.

As I sat on my couch, with tears pouring down my face, I slowly picked up the Bible—with much hesitation—and the pages landed on a story about a man named Nehemiah, who in fifty-two days rebuilt a wall that should have taken years to rebuild. Nothing short of a miracle. According to archaeological records, this wall covered at least thirty acres and lay in ruins for some seventy years. Because of the size, length, and severe damage done to the wall, it should not have been rebuilt in fifty-two days but Nehemiah assembled a team and did it. To that end, I was eager to learn how he did it. I found some amazing principles that I will be unfolding in the next few hours or days I have with you, such as laying a strong foundation, seeing the vision, drafting a few, examining yourself, expecting opposition, identifying your why, and not stopping. Now, your life may not change in fifty-two days, but you will see change if you stay consistent. All you need is motivation and determination. Motivation to start. Determination to finish.

One thing that you may find surprising as you read this book is that I am not asking you to find new material to rebuild the area that is bringing you nightmares. In some cases, I am asking you to use the materials that are before you, materials that you thought could not be used. Remember: The miracle may be in your hands. That is, the answer you need may already be in your possession. Do you think Nehemiah rebuilt the city walls of Jerusalem with new material? He may have used some, but mostly he used what was already there. In truth, Nehemiah already had the gifts to rebuild the walls of Jerusalem inside him but it took a bad report from his brother to wake them up.

We have the wrong perception as it pertains to a setback. We view it as an opportunity for failure. God views a setback as an opportunity for you to see the greatness inside of you.

I believe God has given gifts to all of us to use. Gifts that can bring a future that we could not imagine or think of. Gifts that can help us rebuild through dark times.

There is nothing special about Nehemiah's life. He started at the bottom. But he had the faith to rebuild and it changed his life forever. And I believe the same can happen to you. Are you ready to rebuild? Are you ready to get out of that rut?

Let's rebuild.

You cannot build a dream on a foundation of sand.
To weather the test of storms, it must be cemented
in the heart with uncompromising conviction.

—T. F. Hodge

Step 1

Lay the Foundation

When you elect a leader to do a special task, you do not elect a cup bearer, someone who tastes wine for a king to see if it contains poison or to see if it is good enough for the king. But that is what happened to Nehemiah. He was a wine taster but God chose to use him (Neh. 1:11).

Now, Nehemiah's job did give him the luxury to be in the company of the king. The Persian king trusted Nehemiah because of his faithful service to him. I guess I would too—if you tasted my wine for poison. Besides the fact that he had job security, you and I can agree that he did not have the best job. He is at the bottom. Nehemiah's day would go something like this:

Wake up.

Brush his teeth.

Put on his clothes.

Pour wine.

Taste the wine.

Give it to the king.

Thank God that the wine did not poison him and do it all over again the next day.

Wake up.

Brush his teeth.

Put on his clothes.

Pour wine.

Taste the wine.

Give it to the king.

As Nehemiah is preparing for another day of wine tasting, he is interrupted by a visitor, one of his brothers and some other men from Judah. Nehemiah talks to them and asks how his people, the Jews, were doing (Neh. 1:2).

Listen to the bad report.

They said to me, "Those who survived the exile and are back in the province are in great trouble and disgrace. The wall of Jerusalem is broken down, and its gates have been burned with fire" (Neh. 1:3 New International Version).

Obviously, Nehemiah had been thinking about his kinfolks for a while. And upon finally getting a report about them, he receives this bad news. The broken walls of Jerusalem are a big issue. In Nehemiah's day, it would be like having a house without doors. For a teenager, it would be like having an iPhone without a lock pattern. Without the walls, anyone can come into the city and destroy it. Without the walls, anyone can come in and intrude in your personal space. The walls represented safety and privacy.

After the news, Nehemiah probably had many thoughts run through his head.

How can it be?

Why?

Anyone can hurt them.

Will my kinfolk perish?

I am sure Nehemiah was expecting better news than what he had received.

Can you relate to Nehemiah? To someone giving you a bad report? We all can.

After hearing about his kinfolk, Nehemiah could have flipped out. He could have given up on life altogether. He could have robbed a bank out of anger. But he did not do any of those things.

When I heard these things, I sat down and wept. For some days I *mourned* and fasted and prayed before the God of heaven (Neh. 1:4, emphasis mine).

If you noticed, Nehemiah took some days to mourn. I call it . . .

Trench Digging

When I was child, I would watch my grandfather build brick walls. Needless to say, I respect anyone who builds brick walls for a living. It is not an easy job. There are a lot of steps that go into building a wall, with the beginning stage being trench digging.

The beginning stage would go something like this:

In the hot scorching sun, my grandpa would pick up a shovel and dig out a trench for a foundation. The size of the trench would determine the size of the wall. In other words, the taller the wall, the deeper you would have to dig the trench.

I call Nehemiah's trench digging mourning. How many times has something terrible happened to you and you did not take the time out to mourn? If you do not take time to mourn or trench dig, you will find yourself on an emotional roller coaster. You will be up one day and down the next.

This is a good stage to get out all of the junk so God can pour a strong foundation inside you. Jesus said, "And no one puts new wine into old wineskins. For the new wine would burst the wineskins, spilling the wine and ruining the skins" (Luke 5:37 New Living Translation).

This is a critical stage in the rebuilding process. In fact, you cannot move into a new relationship without letting the old go. If you try to, the old relationship will ruin the new one, even though the old one is long gone.

You cannot have true happiness in the future while holding onto yesterday. Joyce Meyer, one of the world's leading practical Bible teachers, asserts, "There are many people who aren't experiencing victory today because they are focused on yesterday." With this in mind, some aren't going to experience a new life because they are stuck in the past.

After I heard what happened to my brother, I was very angry and lost. A couple of weeks after the accident, my wife gave me some simple but powerful advice. She said, "Curtis, just cry." I replied, "I'm all right."

A couple of days later, I went to the back room by myself and cried my eyes out. It felt so good. It was the beginning of a new life.

I called one of my mentors and he asked me why I felt like I had to be so strong. He told me that grieving is a natural process and I should let the process work. I guess I have a hard time grieving. After the death of my father, I became numb. I shut the door to my feelings. This is not a good thing to do. It will affect your relationships. It is okay to mourn, and I had to learn that. If you have been hurt by a spouse, a friend, or a close relative, take some time to mourn. It will help.

This is your time to dig out all of that hurt and pain. Look inside and ask yourself if there is anything that would hinder you from moving forward. We all have things God would like to purge out of us. If your father walked out of your life, take the time to do deal with it now. If you have been hurt by someone in the past and still holding on to it, take the time to deal with it now. If you were the cause of the financial breakdown in your home, forgive yourself. If you were the cause for your marriage falling apart, forgive yourself.

The more you want to rebuild, the deeper you are going to have to dig. So I want you to dig, dig, and dig some more. Dig until you can look up to the sky and say, "I'm free."

Level Your Emotions

The next thing my grandpa would do is make sure the ground was leveled. He would pick up several stakes and drive them into the ground. He could not move onto the next step unless all stakes were evenly leveled.

Mourning or a time of releasing helps you level your emotions. The first thing Nehemiah did again was grieve. That is the natural thing to do when you receive bad news or something bad happens to you.

It is critical that you take time to grieve. In fact, grieving will jump start the rebuilding process. I did not dedicate an entire chapter to grieving but please take time to do it. The grieving process may take some days, like Nehemiah.

Sometimes we try to play Superman, especially men. We have a tendency to hide our feelings. But I am glad that Nehemiah was vulnerable before God.

Mourning is actually what I did at the hospital. I could not sleep. I could not eat. All the doctors could tell us was that my brother might or might not make it. Only time would tell.

Now you cannot skip this process because you have to make sure that the foundation is level before you move on to actually rebuilding your life. If the foundation is uneven, then the wall will not be stable. I don't care how high the wall is, if the foundation is not strong, the wall will slowly crumble. Some people try to move on with life after a hurt to realize that the same hurt will haunt them like a nightmare.

I do prison ministry once or twice a year. And let me tell you there are some smart, intelligent, talented, and gifted young men in prison who holds the keys to the future. But the keys are locked up behind bars.

As I was ministering to one of the guys, he began to open up and share his story with me. It brought me to tears.

The inmate told me that he was on the honor roll. He could have gone to just about any college, just on his academics alone. But a few weeks before graduation, he made a terrible mistake.

He went on to tell me that his stepfather would brutally beat on his mother. After so many times of watching, he could not take it anymore. He flipped.

He walked into the house, finding his stepfather brutally pounding his mother in the face. He (the inmate) picked up his stepfather's gun and pulled the trigger. He killed his stepfather.

One reaction changed the inmate's future. He had a bright future. He was on his way to becoming a doctor or a lawyer. But one quick reaction changed it all. Stories like this are one of the main reasons why I leave the prison with tears falling down my face like a waterfall.

I shared this story because it shows the importance of leveling your emotions. When we face a devastating situation, the first reaction is to react quickly, without considering the consequences. I believe that is why Nehemiah took some days to level his emotions. I heard one pastor say that emotional people make bad decisions.

Once you start rebuilding there is no going back to make sure the footing is level. There are six words the inmate said over and over again:

"I wish I could go back."

Your emotions need to be leveled before you begin. The last thing I want to see happen to you is to find yourself in a place where you don't belong, like this young man. After my father was murdered, I actually sat in a car for three nights in a row with a gun, contemplating if I was going to go find and kill the person who murdered my father. The murderer shot my father ten times. Needless to say, my emotions were everywhere. I am glad that I took the time to level my emotions because otherwise I probably would have been in prison.

Mix the Mortar

After digging a trench and making sure the ground was leveled, my grandpa would mix the mortar the old school way. He would mix water, Portland Cement, lime, and sand. He would mix all the ingredients until he got his desired result.

That is exactly what Nehemiah did. He did not mix mortar but he mixed prayer and fasting.

Nehemiah said, "For some days I mourned and *fasted* and *prayed* before the God of heaven" (Neh. 1:4, emphasis mine).

Nehemiah prayed an awesome prayer (you can find the entire prayer in Chapter 1). I want to highlight the last verse.

"Lord, let your ear be attentive to the prayer of this your servant and to the prayer of your servants who delight in revering your name. Give your servant success today by granting him favor in the presence of this man" (Neh. 1:11).

Nehemiah wanted to help the Jews but he needed the permission of the king before he could go. This was not an easy request. In fact, Nehemiah was afraid to approach the king (Neh. 2:2). But Nehemiah realized that prayer and fasting would open the door. Nehemiah unplugged from his regular routine of wine tasting and sought after God's presence like never before. And his request to go rebuild the wall was granted as a result.

I don't know how you are feeling. Maybe you just lost a loved one. Maybe your husband walked out on you. Maybe you were promised a promotion but did not get it. Whatever the situation, take some time to fast and pray.

Prayer and fasting still works. Due to the accident, my brother had undergone several surgeries. To make sure his body would heal properly, the doctors advised us to keep him sedated for a week. We did. That was the longest week. My family and I stayed at the hospital around the clock.

A week passed and it was time for the doctors to wake him up. My family and I had waited patiently for a whole week. The time had finally come. Not really.

When the doctors tried to wake him up, nothing happened. My brother was not responding to their call. So they advised us to run some more tests.

I went home for a couple of hours to catch up on a few things. Then my cell phone started to ring. My uncle told me to get back to the hospital. I rushed right out the door and found myself pulling into the parking lot but not parking.

My family was standing at the edge of the sidewalk crying. I parked my car on the curb and jumped out, wondering why everyone was crying. My uncle told me that my brother had lost too much oxygen to his brain due to the accident. In short, there was nothing the doctors could do. The doctors were going to have to pull the plug in five more days.

After I gathered my emotions, I called everyone I knew to put my brother on their prayer list. My family needed God like never before.

As the news traveled, the waiting room became packed with visitors. Some came to hold us and cry with us. Others came to offer a word of prayer. Those were the longest five days of my life.

Tuesday came. My brother was not responding.

Wednesday came. My brother was not responding.

Thursday came. My brother was not responding.

Friday arrived and the doctors gave us till 8:00 p.m. to pull the plug.

The doctor in charge of my brother's case called us into a room to give us the normal goodbye routine. It went something this:

"Take time to spend with Chadwick. He will not make it after we pull the plug. Would you like to donate his organs?" the doctor asked.

The doctor said some other things, but I cannot remember. I was zoned out. I know one thing for sure: when we left the meeting I prayed, prayed, and fasted some more. My family prayed, prayed, and fasted some more. My friends prayed, prayed, and fasted some more.

I did not need a favor from a king like Nehemiah. I needed God to grant my brother more time.

The time to pull the plug came. The doctors allowed the immediate family to come and watch. I cannot explain the emotions that rushed through me while the doctors slowly backed down on the oxygen they were giving my brother.

Each moment they dialed down, my heart dialed down. We had people in the waiting room praying as they were dialing down. We were praying for a miracle to happen.

After the doctor finished dialing the oxygen completely down, everyone waited to see what was going to happen. My family and I witnessed a miracle that night. My brother continued to breathe on his own. Prayer and fasting still work. Jesus said, "This kind can come forth by nothing but by prayer and fasting" (Mark 9:29).

Pray for a specific result. Yes, I am asking you to pray for a specific result before you begin rebuilding. Nehemiah prayed for favor with the king (Neh. 1:11). Nehemiah realized that the king could have turned him down from going to rebuild the walls of Jerusalem. If the king says no, then the whole process is shut down.

That is why I am asking you to pray a specific prayer. Pray for thing you would like to see rebuilt in your life. It may be a relationship. It may be a new job. You may want to be set free from a drug or alcohol addiction. Your prayer would go something like this:

Father, I ask you to help me as I strive to get off drugs. Or Father, I ask you to help me as I strive to rebuild my marriage.

Prayer should be the first thing you do before you embark to rebuild. Not a complex prayer but a simple, straightforward prayer. We will discuss in the following pages what to do after you have prayed, which will consist of action on your part. The Book of James tells us that faith without works is dead (2:14–26). This chapter is simply laying the foundation but the following chapters are all about laying bricks, so get ready.

Before they pulled the plug on my brother, my family and I prayed a specific prayer: that God would allow him to live. And God granted our request. God allowed him to live four more years. It was nothing but a miracle from God, seeing that he died twice, one time on the scene and another time when he arrived at the hospital.

Pour the Concrete

There was one more step my grandpa took before he started laying the bricks: he poured the concrete. I am not asking you to pour concrete but I am asking you to pour your whole heart into the rebuilding process. You have to make up in your mind that you are going to rebuild. Nobody can make that decision for you. I can give the principles to help you but you have to choose to use those principles.

I had to practice a lot of self-discipline to dig out of my hole. Elbert Hubbard once said, "Self-discipline is the ability to do what you should do, when you should do it, whether you feel like it or not."

There are going to be days when you cannot see the light at the end of the tunnel. That is a fact. I am not going to lie to you and tell you that the rebuilding process is going to be a walk in the park. Nope. Not at all.

You are going to have to have the self-discipline to keep going whether you feel like it or not. Brian Tracy, a leading expert on the subject of personal success, noted, "I have discovered that you can achieve almost any goal you set for yourself if you have the discipline to pay the price, to do what you need to do, and to never give up." I am asking you to resolve in your mind that you are going to pay the price, work the steps, and not give up, no matter what.

I have spent so much time on the foundation because, again everything relies on a strong foundation. Since the foundation has been laid, it's time to pick up the bricks and start rebuilding a better you.

THINGS TO REMEMBER

1. Building a strong foundation is the most important step in the rebuilding process, so take the time to put thoughtful consideration into it. The stronger the foundation, the more stable your life will be.

2. Determine in your heart that you are going to dig deep and let go of past hurts. Set yourself free so you can move on with life and see the new you. Resolve in your mind that you are going to give 120 percent to the rebuilding process.

Write a 120% commitment letter to yourself, and answer the following questions:

1. What are you committed to rebuilding?
2. What are you willing to give up in order to see the new you emerge?
3. What are you willing to do in order to succeed?
4. Why do you want to change?
5. What do you see yourself becoming?

Once you have answered those questions arrange your answers into a commitment paragraph. Read your commitment paragraph daily.

Commitment Paragraph

_____

_____

_____

_____

_____

_____

_____

_____

_____

_____

_____

_____

_____

_____

_____

_____

_____

_____

_____

_____

_____

_____

_____

_____

_____

Sign here: _____

Where there is no vision, there is no hope.

—George Washington Carver

Step 2

See the Vision

As I was going through my secretly depressed season, I sat on my couch with tears streaming down my face, and a voice echoed through my mind and touched the inner core of my spirit, saying, "Vision." This word struck something in me like a kid walking into Disney Land for the first time. Rosabeth Kanter observed, "A vision is not just a picture of what could be; it is an appeal to our better selves, a call to become something more." From that moment on, I got it. Curtis, get a vision that's bigger than what you are currently facing. See something bigger and better than sitting on this couch. See yourself becoming more. I have learned that your vision has to become bigger than your reality.

You may have faced a divorce but can you see a better marriage?

You may have lost a job but can you see a better job?

You may be a high school dropout but can you see a degree in your hand?

You may be working at a job you don't like but can you see a better job?

You may have filed bankruptcy but can you see a savings account full of money?

It doesn't matter what you are trying to accomplish in life or whatever you are trying to rebuild, it is going to take a vision to climb out of that hole. Taking a few minutes to see a vision beyond your current circumstances, can give you hope to move from where you are to where you need to be. Steve Jobs, cofounder of Apple and one of the greatest innovators to ever live, said, "If you are working on something exciting that you really care about, you don't have to be pushed. The vision pulls you." Rebuilding is an exciting time but you must see a vision of doing it.

I am not telling you something that I do not believe in or have not tried in my own life. I was riding in the car with one of my great friends. I told him that I would achieve a higher education degree someday. This is when I had no high school diploma. No proof, just vision. Now I am two to three years from making that happen. I am currently working on my doctoral dissertation, so trust me when I tell you this: Vision is powerful. Your imagination is one of the greatest gifts God has given you. No one can take it from you, nor can anyone stop the measure of your imagination. Steve Harvey, in his book *Act Like a Success Think Like a Success*, said, "My vision board helps me to let my imagination go, push every boundary out of the way, and get tuned in to my gift and purpose for being here on Earth."

There is a story in the Bible about a man named Abraham, who can bring this principle of seeing the vision to life. Abraham is doing life as usual. But God approaches him and tells him to leave his country and his people and go to a land that he will show him. Not a lot of instructions, just a "go" and a vision:

"I will make you into a great nation, and I will bless you; I will make your name great, and you will be a blessing. I will bless those who bless you, and whoever curses you I will curse; and all peoples on earth will be blessed through you" (Gen. 12:2–3).

Do you see the vision God gave Abraham? The vision was calling Abraham to become something more. It was calling him out of his current circumstances and into something greater.

But there was one problem: Abraham could not see the vision. So God helped him. The writer of Genesis says, "He [God] took him [Abraham] outside and said, "Look up at the sky and count the stars—if indeed you can count them." Then he said to him, "So shall your offspring be" (Gen. 15:5). Abraham did not have any kids at the time, but God was giving him a vision to see, a future to believe in.

This is what I want you to do before you try to rebuild. Find a vision that's bigger than yourself, a vision that will demand that you become something more.

As I was watching television, I found myself glued to a video by Les Brown, one of the greatest motivational speakers living.

Les told the crowd that even when he was broke and sleeping on floors, he believed that he would be speaking around the world one day. Even though he was considered educable mentally retarded, he would become a motivational speaker. When he watched someone speak on TV, he visualized that he would be doing the same thing. He actually took a picture of himself and placed it on the top right corner of his television screen. And the rest, as they say, is history. Les is doing what he saw himself doing because he saw the vision.

I don't know where you are in your life right now. You may be reading this from a prison cell. You may have just filed bankruptcy and are worried about how you are going to rebuild your life. No matter where you are this principle applies to everyone. It is free. It takes vision to rebuild.

I have read numerous leadership and personal growth books. The books in my library have one theme in common, no matter the subject: people who have achieved or rebounded from bad circumstances started with a vision.

God gave Abraham a vision of an offspring. Les Brown had vision of being on television. Nehemiah had vision to see the walls of Jerusalem rebuilt. In all three cases:

No materials yet, just vision.

No team yet, just vision.

Whatever you are endeavoring to rebuild, you need a vision and . . .

See It Complete

After my grandpa came home from work one day, I asked him how he managed to build a brick wall. He replied, "I see the wall complete before I start." Likewise, you have to see your situation complete before you start. Whenever I want to write a book, I make up a graphic that I can look at every day. This graphic reminds me of a finished product although it is not complete. It gives me drive. It invigorates my passion to keep writing. Bishop TD Jakes, one of the most influential leaders in America today, commented, "You cannot be what you do not see."

Michelangelo was an Italian sculptor in the 1500s who made a 14.0 ft marble statue of the Old Testament Hero King David. His marble statue is still one of the greatest masterpieces ever. Of course, Michelangelo was asked how he did the statue, which took him two years to finish.

Michelangelo gave them a simple answer: "I saw the statue complete before I started. I just had to chip away anything that did not look like the finished product." You have to see the vision of the new you complete before you start your journey of rebuilding and then chip away anything that does not look like it, which we will learn about in the examination process later.

Keep It a Secret

In the Old Testament, God had given a young man by the name of Joseph two dreams. Both dreams indicated that he would be a great leader.

Like most of us, when Joseph received the good news, he told his brothers and family. There is nothing wrong with sharing some good news but some news should stay between you and God until the appropriate time. Because Joseph shared his dreams with his brothers, they hated him.

There is no worse feeling than sharing a vision or dream with someone and he or she gives you the screw face.

Nehemiah did the smart thing. Instead of posting it on Facebook or tweeting about it, when Nehemiah arrived in Jerusalem, he did not tell anyone what God had put in his heart:

"I set out during the night with a few others. I had not told anyone what my God had put in my heart to do for Jerusalem" (Neh. 2:12).

I was having lunch with someone and I began to open my heart and share with this person some things I believed God was calling me to do.

Over the next few minutes all I heard was negativity, negativity that almost altered my future.

I want you to keep it a secret. Nobody needs to know what you are working on.

Your vision is too precious for it to be hindered by negative words.

While Michelangelo was working on his best sculpture, he hid from everyone. Why? He did not want to be bothered, for one thing. Another reason is he understood the power of negative words. You have to protect your vision. People will say you can't do something to stop you from becoming great.

You are going to have a chance to go public with your vision but for right now I want you to keep it a secret.

Give It Time to Marinate

I enjoy my wife's cooking but I mostly enjoy her slow cooking roast in the crock pot. Man, I can smell and taste it as I am writing this page. When you slow cook your food, the taste just goes to another level. I prefer crockpot over the microwave anytime of the day. It is true; you can warm your food up a lot faster in the microwave but the taste is not the same.

One main reason why my wife's pot roast tastes so delicious is because she allows the meat time to soak in a marinade.

Yes, I am asking you to give your vision time to soak.

Nehemiah did.

When Nehemiah arrived in Jerusalem, he stayed there for three days before he did anything. Why? He was given the vision some more time to marinate.

This idea may sound bizarre. But if you do not give the vision time to soak inside your heart, you will not be ready for the opposition that is coming.

Before you start building a brick wall you have to lay the footings and then allow it to dry for a few days before starting the building process. Needless to say, it is an important step.

When your vision becomes a part of you, no one, and I mean no one, can stop you. Nehemiah said the vision was in his heart (Neh. 2:12). When Jesus Christ came to the earth, He had a vision in His heart: to bring the kingdom of God to the earth and to die for all mankind. Nothing and no one could stop Him from accomplishing that. He had it in his heart. Even when one of his disciples tried to hinder Him, look at what He said:

Jesus turned and said to Peter, "Get behind me, Satan! You are a stumbling block to me; you do not have in mind the concerns of God, but merely human concerns" (Matt. 16:23).

Until you have this kind of attitude, it is not in your heart. Until you have a vision that excites you, it is not in your heart. Until you have a vision that keeps you up at night, it is not in your heart.

Do you have a vision to rebuild? If so, now I need you to take it out of your mind and put it on paper. Go ahead and grab a pen and let's start writing.

Put It on Paper

Whatever you would like to see happen in your life, write it down on paper. I found that people who wrote their vision down on paper had almost a 50 percent better chance of achieving it than the ones who did not. Even more astounding is below five percent of adults actually have written down on paper what they want in life. This will help you to stay focused on the one thing you want to rebuild instead of trying to juggle multiple things at one time. I just want you to put your vision on paper at this time. We will discuss later how to break it down into small steps so you can take them one by one until you see the new you.

There was a prophet by the name of Habakkuk who was living in terrible times, worse than what we are currently living in. God instructed Habakkuk to write down the vision that he would like to see:

And the LORD answered me: "Write the vision; make it plain on tablets, so he may run who reads it" (Hab. 2:2 English Standard Version).

I want you to write the vision down because when you can see it every day on paper, it will help you do three things:

Vision will help you stay focused. The first time I took my family to the beach I went off course—about an hour off course. My wife said, "Do you know where you are going?" I replied, "Yes." Thirty minutes later, she suggested I stop and ask for help.

After an hour of extra driving, I finally stopped and pulled into a convenience store and asked for help. To my surprise (*not really*), I was driving in the wrong direction.

The next year we went back to the same spot but I did something totally different: I purchased a GPS system. What a lifesaver!

What was interesting about the GPS is that every time I got off course, it would kindly guide me back on track.

Vision works the same way when you write it on paper. When you have a vision, your mind will not allow you to go off track for long. For example, if your vision is to rebuild your health, your mind will scream at you every time you try to scarf down a honey bun. If you have a vision to rebuild your finances, your mind will scream at you when you spend too much. If you have a vision to make good grades, your mind will remind you that you are not spending enough time studying. In short, vision will keep you focused and on track toward the big picture. Nehemiah faced opposition but the vision to rebuild the walls of Jerusalem propelled him forward.

Vision will help you say no. Your time is valuable. After you write down a vision for your life, there are going to be a lot of things trying to take your time but when you have a vision written down, you can screen out the things that do not need to be there. We waste too much time, time that we cannot get back. For instance, say you want to make better grades in school and your friends ask you to go to a party but you know you need to study. Because of the peer pressure, you go to the party. The next morning you fail the test. Now you wish you could go back but you cannot. But if you had that vision written down you could have observed it and said this party is not worth my time. Vision will help you say no. Jesus told Peter no.

Vision will help you find what is important. Not only will vision help you say no; it will help you find what's important. Although you may think everything in your life is important, it is not. Time to do a checklist. We learn it in school but as we grow older we forget about the checklist. When you write down your vision, it will help you determine what's important and what's not. For example, I am a writer. I am a speaker. So I read books focused on those subjects. If someone asked me to read a book on music lessons, I would tell them no thank you. Why? Because it is not important to me or my time but even more importantly, it does not line up with my vision. I'd rather say no. Now that you have a foundation and you have a vision for what you would like to see, it is time to draft a few friends to go on the journey with you.

THINGS TO REMEMBER

1. Take the time to sit down and get a vision for your life, if you don't already have one. Don't put a limit on your vision. All things are possible with God. Your vision is precious so protect it and do not let outsiders harm it. Treat it like a new born. Protect it. Nurture it. And one day it will grow into its full potential.

2. Your vision has to move beyond your mind and onto paper. When you write it down, your mind will store it and remind you daily of what you are rebuilding. If other activities do not line up with your vision, slowly let them go. You only have one life to live and one vision to pursue, so manage your time wisely. Let unproductive activities go. Every rebuilding story started with a vision.

No person is your friend who demands your silence, or denies your right to grow.

—Alice Walker

Step 3

Draft a Few

I don't watch a lot of sports but I do watch football. This particular day I was watching the NFL draft. I understand the concept behind the draft but I don't understand why only a few get drafted. I mean, you have players that have given their whole life for this one moment, a chance to make it to the NFL, but they go undrafted.

Nehemiah understood the idea of drafting a few. No matter how many we think we need for the journey, only a few really matter. No matter how many things we think we need for the journey, only a few matter. When Nehemiah decided to rebuild the wall, he drafted a few.

I set out during the night with a few others. I had not told anyone what my God had put in my heart to do for Jerusalem. There were no mounts with me except the one I was riding on. (Neh. 2:12, emphasis mine)

Nehemiah set out during the night with a few others. It amazes me how many people we let in our inner circle, especially when we are trying to rebuild. It is time to draft a few. So how do you go about drafting a few? How do you know which friends to put on your team? I am glad you asked because I want to help you.

Scouting

Before the draft, NFL teams send scouts out to find the best players around the world. They spend thousands of dollars to find the best players. They stay in hotels for many nights to find the best players. All of this for one or two draft picks. Why don't we use the same energy when picking our inner circle?

The scouts find the best players that they think will fit into their organization's values and mission. They look for players they think will take them to the Super Bowl. Likewise, it is time for you to go scout hunting for friends that align with your values and mission, friends that will help you get to your destination—not the Super Bowl, but the new you.

Jesus believed in the idea of drafting a few. He had an idea to change the world but only chose twelve unqualified people to do it with. He could have chosen anyone in the world but he took the time to find twelve people he could fulfill his mission with. Jesus took time to scout out these guys. Some were fishermen. One of them was a tax collector. Jesus actually spent the night praying before he chose the people he drafted to put on his team (Luke 6:12).

You will not be able to rebuild by yourself. You are going to need support. But draft a few. Nehemiah could have chosen a lot of people but he chose a few to put in his inner circle as well. Here are a few things to look for when you are scouting.

Are They Doing Something?

When scouts go out to observe, they look to see if the players are doing something. When Jesus chose the twelve disciples all of them were doing something. When Elijah, an Old Testament prophet, went to find Elisha to replace him as the new prophet, he was plowing oxen.

You need to draft friends who are doing something, friends that have goals and dreams. You do not need people that are going to drain you. It is hard to rebuild when you are trying to find energy to rebuild yourself but you are constantly being drained.

Do They Have Your Best Interests in Mind?

When Nehemiah arrived in Jerusalem, he chose a few people who had his best interests in mind. Some people will be out to get you so you have to be diligent in finding a few that have your best interests in mind. Ask yourself this question: Do they believe in what you are trying to rebuild? If not, then you need to keep looking.

I am not talking about "yes" friends. You need some "no" friends, friends that can look you straight in the eye and tell you the truth. I am reminded of American Idol. Simon Cowell did not mind telling the contestants the truth, although it hurt their feelings. Don't mix passion with purpose. A lot of people came on American Idol with a passion to sing but the truth is they could not. You need friends that can differentiate between the two as well.

When I was working on the introduction for this book, I asked a friend to tell me what he thought. He insisted that I make a few minor adjustments and I did. He could have been a "yes" friend and allowed me to produce an ineffective introduction but he did not mind correcting me because he had my best interest in mind.

Are They Willing to Hold Your Ladder?

You heard me correctly. Find friends who are willing to hold your ladder. In the process of rebuilding your life, you are going to be going up, not down. So you need friends who do not mind seeing you climb the ladder of life. These friends are going to hold your ladder steady while you climb to the top. You don't need friends who are going to push your ladder while you are trying to climb. It makes the climb that much harder.

The only things you need to be hearing while you are climbing are positive words:

You can do it.

Just one more step.

You are almost at the top.

Don't look down because we have your back.

These are the type of people you need holding your ladder. You may have to climb down a few times but true friends will be there to tell you to get back on that ladder and keep rebuilding.

I became very frustrated while writing this book, especially when I had written for several hours for no reason. I went to the coffee shop to write and I mean I had some amazing thoughts flow through that day. If you are a writer, you understand what I am talking about. When the creative juices are flowing, you stay in that moment. I got home later that day and was about to show my wife all the good ideas I had written that day. I opened my laptop and nothing was there. I mean nothing but what I had written days before.

I forgot to hit the save button. I almost cried. I wanted to give up. I believe my wife saw the anger in my eyes and walked over to me and told me that I was going to write it even better this time and that I could rebuild. And I did.

Nehemiah went to Jerusalem and found a few people to hold his ladder. Be careful who you let hold your ladder. If their life is unstable, then they do not need to be holding your ladder. Take time to scout out the best players to put on your team.

After you have found a few draft picks, that is not the end. Now, you have to send them through a workout. This workout will determine if they truly have what it takes.

Scouting Combine

The NFL scouting combine is a week-long process where college players perform physical tests to see if they have what it takes to make it to the draft. They also go through mental tests. NFL scouting combine calls them drills.

Likewise, you need to send the few you have selected through a physical and mental test. Remember: these are the friends who will be helping you rebuild, so you need some friends who can stand through the worst of times.

You may be asking how? Easy. Start by telling him or her something, something that you don't mind getting back to you. If the secret makes it back full circle, he or she has failed the secret drill.

Try the encouragement drill. When you call him or her, do they have something encouraging to say or does he or she say negative things constantly? The accountability drill is one of the biggest drills. Let's say you decide to give up in the middle of rebuilding your life. Will they hold you accountable and tell you to get back on the ladder or sing the sad song, "It's okay. Take a rest"? You do not have time to take a rest. You need to stay on the ladder and keep climbing. You don't need friends who are going to let you revert to your old ways. My wife held me accountable when I wanted to give up on writing this book. You can create your own drills moving forward but I have given you a jump start: encouragement drill, secret drill, and the accountability drill.

Draft Day

When NFL draft day comes, the NFL teams, which consist of thirty-two clubs, have seven rounds to pick a player each round. This is a crucial process because they have to determine who deserves to be on the team, which players have given their best.

It is draft day for you. You have seven rounds to pick some friends to move forward with. You cannot make this journey alone. You need friends. You need support. Look through your list of names and make your first and second round picks. Your spouse should be number one so I have given the first round pick.

Round one:

Make rounds one and two your best picks. These people will become starters. They will have a clear window to look into your life. They will more than likely become lifelong friends. They get the biggest contracts. Your round one and round two friends will be holding your ladder steady.

Now it is time to look into your roster again.

Round two:

Have you filled in the blank yet? If so, congratulations! These two draft picks are critical to your growth. Thank them for joining your team.

Make a Trade

Sometimes NFL teams will make trades throughout the draft. Likewise, don't be afraid to make trades. Just because you drafted them to be on your team now does not mean that they will be there later.

I have one close friend who has been there for me for a long time and some who have slowly faded out of my life. When my family and I moved to Greensboro, North Carolina, I needed to find some more friends. So guess what I did? I scouted out some. I sent them through the drill test. Only two passed. They are now on my team with my other friends. Don't be afraid to make trades. The people in your life may not be the people you need to help you rebuild.

Only two people can hold your ladder, so the other five draft picks will be there for encouragement. They are looking into your life from a different viewpoint. The two holding your ladder see you from the bottom. They know all your hurt and dirt but still don't mind holding your ladder. The other five are standing from a distance and they have the end in mind. They see what's at the top of your ladder: the new you. They are your encouragers. So now it is time to look back at the roster and draft five more.

Draft three:

Draft four:

Draft five:

Draft six:

Draft seven:

I am glad your roster is full. If it is not, don't panic. You have time to fill your roster. But I would encourage you to find two people who will be there to walk beside you. Albert Camus asserts, "Don't walk in front of me . . . I may not follow. Don't walk behind me . . . I may not lead. Walk beside me . . . just be my friend." This quote sums up what friendship and this chapter is all about: drafting a few that will walk beside you, no matter what you are going through.

You have laid a foundation. You have the vision. You have drafted a few to go on the journey with. Now, it is time to examine those broken down walls.

THINGS TO REMEMBER

1. You will not be able to travel the road to rebuilding by yourself. You are going to need help and support. God created us to be in relationships so we can strengthen one another. Draft two friends who can hold your ladder as you climb. These two friends are important to your rebuilding process.

2. Be careful who you choose to be on your team. Walk through the crowd slowly and find people who have dreams and goals. Find people who align with your values.

Know who you are, and be it. Know what you
want, and go out and get it!

—Carroll Bryant

Step 4

Examination

I am glad you have made it this far in the book. This step is going to take a little more effort. When Nehemiah arrived in Jerusalem, he examined the walls. He carefully studied the situation before he began. Literally, he spent several days observing the broken down walls in Jerusalem.

In his examination, he saw what he could use, what he could not use, and how he could use the new material he brought with him to rebuild on the ruins that were left. This is a crucial step to rebuilding a better you. You have the foundation. You have a vision. You have selected a few to be in your inner circle. Now you have to sit down and plan. Lailah Akita, in *Pearls of Wisdom*, found that "If you fail an examination, it means you have not yet mastered the subject. With diligent study and understanding, you will succeed in passing the exams."

I believe the same truth applies to whatever you are trying to rebuild. You need to take the time to study whatever you are trying to rebuild so you can succeed. Nehemiah took time to study or examine the area in which he was endeavoring to rebuild:

By night I went out through the Valley Gate toward the Jackal Well and the Dung Gate, *examining* the walls of Jerusalem, which had been broken down, and its gates, which had been destroyed by fire. Then I moved on toward the Fountain Gate and the King's Pool, but there was not enough room for my mount to get through; so I went up the valley by night, *examining* the wall. Finally, I turned back and reentered through the Valley Gate. (Neh. 2:13–15 NIV, emphasis mine)

As you can see through this scripture, Nehemiah put thoughtful consideration into rebuilding the walls. I am going to give you six things that have helped me when I was examining my situation. Dwight Eisenhower says, "Plans are nothing; planning is everything." You are about to put wheels on your vision. You are about to create a roadmap.

Step one: *Find out what you are aiming for.* You have to have a target you are shooting toward. I don't know if you have experienced depression but it is a dark place to be in. To literally dig yourself out, you have to find something positive to aim for. I have always been a positive person. But after the accident happened to my brother, I felt myself turning into something I can't even describe.

During this time, I sat down and found a new Curtis, a Curtis that could smile and be happy again. This is the image I put in my mind that I wanted to aim for. Not the old grumpy, depressed, wishing the world would come to an end Curtis I was slowly becoming. Now find out what you are aiming for. Look back at the vision you wrote down for yourself from chapter 2. If you have not written down anything to aim for, let me give you some examples. For example, it may be to go back to college. Or it may be to purchase a new car. Or perhaps you want to get out of debt. It may be to see your marriage restored. Nehemiah knew what he was aiming for: the wall of Jerusalem being rebuilt.

Step two: *Create an endpoint.* When I speak of an endpoint, I am talking about a deadline. Deadlines will help you take action immediately. People always ask me how to write a book. I tell them to start writing and create an endpoint. The endpoint will give you urgency to start on the rebuilding process now. For example, let's say you are trying to rebuild your health. Without a deadline, you will procrastinate and get nothing done. Creating an endpoint has helped me tremendously. It has helped me start immediately and stay on task.

Nehemiah rebuilt the walls of Jerusalem in fifty-two days. I believe it would be safe to say that he had an endpoint in mind. In fact, the Bible tells us he had an endpoint.

Then the king, with the queen sitting beside him, asked me, "How long will your journey take, and when will you get back?" It pleased the king to send me; *so I set a time.* (Neh. 2:6, emphasis mine)

Nehemiah said, "So I set a time." I believe Nehemiah rebuilt the walls so fast because he set a time, an endpoint. It created an urgency for Nehemiah to start immediately. Say to yourself that in ninety days your marriage is going to be restored. Say to yourself that in ninety days, you will be over this addiction. Set a time and move forward in faith. Even though you may not finish before your deadline, you will be a lot closer to finishing than if you did not have one. In most cases, you will get done early.

Step three: *Gather extra material.* Before Nehemiah left Jerusalem, he asked the king for material. Now, you see him observing to see if he needs more material and what material he does not need. Write down some things you think you are going to need to get the job done. The worst thing that can happen to you while you are on a road trip is to not properly prepare. You would not leave the spare tire at home if you are going on a road trip so don't leave it behind as you are rebuilding your life. For example, some materials you may need are reading extra books or listening to more positive music.

As I was on my journey of rebuilding a better me, I went to Barnes and Noble and purchased several books. Some books were on attitude and others discussed personal growth tips, such as time management. I also created a play list on YouTube that I could listen to for growth. These things helped me tremendously. Find some extra materials to pack.

Step four: *Think about what you already have.* Nehemiah also observed the material that was already there. He found hope in some of the broken pieces. What others marked as lost, Nehemiah marked as gain. To this end, some material may be already there.

I love watching *The Ten Commandments*, especially the encounter Moses has with God at the burning bush. God asked Moses to go free His people from Pharaoh, not an easy task. The children of Israel had been working for Pharaoh for at least four hundred years; well, they were in slavery for at least four hundred years. So Pharaoh had stock in the children of Israel. For Moses to go demand for him to let God's people go was a death sentence to say the least.

After God asked Moses to go, he made several excuses. What caught my eye is how God responded to Moses's insecurities. He asked Moses what he had in his hand, which was a staff. God did not ask Moses if he needed finances for the journey or a horse to ride on. He asked Moses what he had in his hand.

In other words, God was letting Moses know that the answer to Pharaoh letting his people go was in his hand. The miracle had been in his hand the whole time but Moses did not see the potential in it. Moses looked at the staff as something to guide his sheep with or a tool to kill snakes with. God saw it as a tool to free his people.

As I was going through my garage the other day, I found a notebook full of poems and songs I had written in middle school and high school. I even tried to start writing a book in high school called the *Joshua Generation* but I did not get too far. Now that I think about it, the gift to write has always been in me but I did not realize it. Writing has helped me rebuild.

What's in your possession that can be used to help rebuild your life? If you are trying to rebuild your finances, a new job may not be the answer. Maybe the current job you have with a new budget may be the answer. Nehemiah had several leadership qualities in him before he got to Jerusalem, like administration, character, motivation, and persistence.

Step five: *Think about what you don't need.* There are some things you don't need that you think you need. Let the bad things go. Think about the things that make you negative. If you are trying to get back into shape, you would need to get rid of snacks that contain a lot of sugar. If you are trying to stop selling drugs, then you would need to change your environment. If you are trying to finish school, then you might need to reduce extra entertainment, such as going out to parties.

Let me ask you a question: If you were going on a hiking trip and you could only carry one item, what would it be? The other things that you would leave behind are irrelevant compared to the one thing you would carry. Now think about what you can let go that would hinder you from moving forward. It may be a bad attitude. It may be a bad habit of gossiping.

There is a story in the Bible about a man named Gideon, who was about to go to war with thirty-two thousand men. However, God told Gideon to reduce his army down to three hundred. On the outside, this looks crazy. But God knew that Gideon did not need all those men to win the battle he was about to fight. God told Gideon to examine the true fighters from the fake ones through different scenarios. Only three hundred stood the test. Gideon won the battle with three hundred men. Thirty-two thousand reduced down to three hundred.

I want you to think about what you don't need. Like Gideon, we must recognize the danger of trying to carry too much. Some things are better left behind, like 31,700 men Gideon needed to leave behind. If you are trying to stop drinking, then leaving behind your drinking buddies may be a good idea.

Step six: *First things first.* It is time to organize. Think about what needs to be first and what needs to be last on your list. Say you wanted to lose weight. One of the first things on your list should be to work out in the mornings. TV time should not come before workout time. Say you wanted to improve your grades. One of the first things on your list should be to study. Social media should not come before study time. Say you wanted to improve a relationship. Going fishing with the buddies should not come before the relationship you are trying to make stronger. You have to put first things first.

The Pareto principle, by Vilfredo Pareto, helped me with this step. The Pareto principle says that 20 percent of what you do will produce 80 percent of your results. Did you hear what I just said? Twenty percent of your input will account for 80 percent of your return! Now as you organize your list of ten things for example, just realize that two of those things are going to give you more return. So put the things that are not going to give you a good return at the bottom of the list.

I came across a story about a young woman by the name of Lisa Falzone who put first things first. Lisa had a dream of starting a business but could never find the time to do it because of the demands of her job so she had to put her dream at the bottom of the list. As she was moving a sofa, she suffered a back injury that left her bedridden for months. Since she had always wanted to start a company, during this time she was able move her dream to the top of the list. The business idea is called Revel Systems. Today, the company is worth five hundred million dollars.

Because of the back injury, Lisa was able to put first things first. She was able to spend time working on her dream idea and as they say, "The rest is history." Think of the return Lisa Falzone received because she put first things first!

Now think about the vision you want to see happen. Then break it down into small steps, putting first things first. And then begin to take small steps. As you begin to take small steps, I want you to remember to . . .

Clean Out the Closet

As I was cleaning up my house the other day, I decided to go clean my closet. I looked at all the clothes on the hangers, clothes that I have not worn in years. Something spoke to me and said, "You don't have room to put anything new because the old is taking up all the space."

With this in mind, it is time to take some old habits off the hangers so you can hang up some new ones. This is a tough step because your flesh is satisfied with where you are right now but the moment you make a decision to rebuild, your flesh is going to act up. I want you to sit down and think of any bad habits, habits that must go now. For instance, I had a bad habit of waiting to do things. It is called procrastination. However, I learned to put first things first. If I had a paper due, I worked on it first thing in the morning instead of waiting. We all are going to procrastinate. We have to start procrastinating on the things that offer little return instead of pushing off the things that produce more fruit.

If you skip over this step, this book will do you no good. You have to be honest with yourself. You are going to have to look into the mirror and tell yourself, "It is time to change. It is time to rebuild." The habits you have now will not take you into tomorrow. You need a new way of thinking and doing things.

Examine New Habits

Now, I want you to find someone who is already at the point where you are trying to be, the new you. And then examine their habits and begin to implement them into your life. For instance, I wanted to become a good leader. So I started reading leadership books and discovered that Dr. John Maxwell is a leadership expert. Every extra dime I got, I would go to the local book store and purchase one of his books. Then I realized that I had to do more than read his books; I had to learn his habits. If I learned his habits, then I would be one step closer to becoming a better leader.

In one of his books, he talked about what he does every day. John said that he reads, writes, files, thinks, and ask questions. What a habit to have! So I started to do the same thing. Every day, I read, write, file, think, and ask questions. This habit has changed my life.

Warren Buffett, most successful investor in the world asserts, "I insist on a lot of time being spent, almost every day, to just sit and think. That is very uncommon in American business. I read and think. So I do more reading and thinking, and make less impulse decisions than most people in business. I do it because I like this kind of life." Do you see the same pattern in John Maxwell and Warren Buffett? Both, successful men in their own way, take the time to sit, read, and think. In order to rebuild you have to create new habits to replace your old ones. Find a pattern to follow.

What if you are one habit away from changing your life? What is the one new habit you need to pick up? Before I wrote my first book, I was terrified. Why? Because I hadn't learned the pattern to writing books. I watched several videos on writing books and one author said not to worry about anything but writing. The only thing I needed to worry about was writing fifteen minutes a day. This was all I had to do to write a book? Yes. It is true. If you can create the habit of writing for fifteen minutes a day, you can write a book.

Please take the time to find a new pattern to follow. Let go of the old habits that are hindering you. Start replacing them with new habits one by one. Before you know it, you will start to see the new you rise up.

I don't care how far you have fallen, the principle of "habit replacement" can change your life and help you rebuild. Try it. If you read the life stories of successful athletes, you will find a similar pattern. If you listen to the stories of successful marriages, you will find a pattern. If you listen to the stories of people who have rebounded from depression, bankruptcy, or abuse, you will find a similar pattern. If you can't find the pattern, I want you to examine some more.

After I finished my undergrad degree, I thought about not going to grad school because I had heard so many horror stories.

It is too hard.

You can't make it.

You have to write too much.

The research is too hard.

So you know what I did after I learned the principle of habit replacement? I learned the habits of people who had completed grad school and followed their patterns. My undergrad habits would not carry me through grad school.

I finished my master's program with a better GPA than my undergrad program. In fact, seven points higher. When someone tells you can't do something, you can't rebuild, you say, "Yes I can." You just need to examine, find the patterns, and begin to implement them into your life.

Here are seven examples of good habits you want to implement in place of bad habits you'd like to avoid.

Old Habits you want to diminish	New Habits you want to develop
Laziness	Hardworking
Procrastination	Put first things first
Stress	Plan your day, week, and month.
Thinking only negative thoughts	Think positive thoughts
Hanging on to past hurts	Let go of past hurts
See bad in people	See good in people
Depressed	Enjoy life

At this point, going public with your plan to rebuild is still not a good idea. Nehemiah "*said nothing* to the Jews or the priests or nobles or officials or any others who would be doing the work" (Neh. 3:16, emphasis mine).

In the next chapter, you will begin to move forward. Things are going to begin to get intense. The enemy is very happy when you are sitting still and not doing anything with your life. But the moment you decide to take action and rebuild, he comes in like a flood. Don't react when bad things happen while you are rebuilding. The next chapter is going to teach you how to respond to opposition. Time to go public. You have a foundation. You see the vision. You have drafted a few friends to support you. You have planned carefully. Now it is time to take steps to rebuild and expect opposition.

THINGS TO REMEMBER

1. Take the time to plan carefully. Examine your life. Let go of old habits that would hinder you from moving forward and replace them with new habits. These new habits can be found in people who have already become what you are trying to become. The new habits are no good unless you implement them into your life.

2. Create a sense of urgency to get things done. Don't procrastinate on things that need to be done right away. Put first things first. Go and find extra material to use as you are rebuilding. Become a life-long student to the things you are trying to rebuild.

You will face your greatest opposition when you are closest to your biggest miracle.

—Shannon Alder

Step 5

Expect Opposition

The moment you take the first step to rebuilding your life, I want you to expect opposition. Trust me, it is coming. Every time I have tried to move forward in my life some level of opposition occurred. At first, I did not know how to deal with it so I reacted. I remember getting so angry one time after my father was murdered that I said some very bad words to a preacher. In another case, I walked out in the middle of a church service. That is not good. You cannot react. You have to learn how to respond to opposition, like I do now. Don't give the enemy any air time. You are only on this earth for so many minutes. Every minute you spend arguing or complaining, you lose. You cannot get it back. However, you can fight a battle with more confidence when you know how to respond to it.

As soon as Nehemiah announced that he was going to rebuild the wall, opposition started.

Announcement: "Then I said to them, 'You see the trouble we are in: Jerusalem lies in ruins, and its gates have been burned with fire. Come, let us rebuild the wall of Jerusalem, and we will no longer be in disgrace.' I also told them about the gracious hand of my God on me and what the king had said to me. They replied, 'Let us start rebuilding.' So they began this good work" (Neh. 2:17–18).

Opposition: "But when Sanballat the Horonite, Tobiah the Ammonite official and Geshem the Arab heard about it, they mocked and ridiculed us. 'What is this you are doing?' they asked. 'Are you rebelling against the king?'" (Neh. 2:20)

They mocked and ridiculed Nehemiah and his team. So don't be surprised if your haters begin to mock and ridicule you. Use it as strength instead of letting it tear you down. When opposition arises, it is an indication that you are on the right path. God will use the opposition to help you get to the next level. In fact, the Bible says that he will make your enemies a footstool (Luke 20:43). Every level of opposition you step over means you are going higher and higher. This is what happened to Nehemiah. Each new phase of rebuilding the wall, birthed a new level of opposition. What I like about Nehemiah is that he did not react. He did not give his haters any airtime.

Listen, I know what it feels like to be treated poorly. I know what it feels like for someone you love to be taken from you. I know what it feels like to be used. I know what it feels like to want to get back at the enemy. I know what it feels like to want to bless someone out. I know what it feels like to be at the bottom. I know what it feels like to want to give up on life. It does no good to react when someone comes against you in a negative way or when something bad happens to you. Reacting is a waste of time but responding in a positive way will help you rebuild.

Respond with the Source

When Nehemiah faced his first opposition, he responded with the source. He replied, "The God of heaven will give us success" (Neh. 2:20). Nehemiah did not sit there and argue with his haters. He made the response and started rebuilding. Nehemiah understood that God wanted the restoration of the city walls done and if he had God (the source) on his side, nothing or no one could stop him. I believe the Apostle Paul read Nehemiah's story because of how he responded when he faced opposition in the New Testament: "What, then, shall we say in response to these things? If God is for us, who can be against us?" (Rom. 8:31)

This is the type of attitude I want you to carry from this day forward, an attitude that God will give you success and that he is on your side. I want you to consider the source. Just like God wanted to see the restoration of the city walls, he wants to see restoration happen in your life. You will have success if you trust him. It may not look like it at the beginning but victory will come because what God begins, he finishes. Paul said, "Being confident of this, that he who began a good work in you will carry it on to completion until the day of Christ Jesus" (Phil. 1:6).

The enemy is afraid of God. Every time the enemy encountered Jesus in the New Testament, he (the enemy) always bowed in his presence. The source is bigger and stronger than anything you will encounter.

The source can walk on water.

The source spoke the universe into existence.

The source calms storms with a whisper.

The source makes mountains tremble.

When you respond with the source, he will fight on your behalf. In 2 Chronicles, we read, "But you will not even need to fight. Take your positions; then stand still and watch the LORD's victory" (20:17). This is exactly what Nehemiah did. He took his position, called on the source, and watched the Lord's victory. Joel Osteen asserts, "When you have difficulties, don't talk about your problems, talk about your God."

When opposition comes into your life, consider the source (God) and talk about Him. He is powerful. He is faithful. He is all-knowing.

Respond with Prayer

As Nehemiah continued to rebuild the city walls, more opposition came: "When Sanballat heard that we were rebuilding the wall, he became angry and was greatly incensed. He ridiculed the Jews" (Neh. 4:1). But this time Nehemiah responded differently. He responded with prayer (Neh. 4:4–5). When haters begin to gossip about you, it is not worth your time trying to fight them on your own. Pray and let God take care of them. In the Book of Exodus, we read, "the LORD will fight for you; you need only to be still" (14:14).

When you are ridiculed, like Nehemiah, it can cause discouragement. Sanballat and Tobiah tried to mock Nehemiah and his team so they would lose focus on the task at hand. However, Nehemiah did not stand there and trade insults with them. He continued to rebuild the wall. I want you to do the same thing. I want you to pray (give God your haters) and continue to rebuild your life. Don't feel like you have to be spiritually deep to pray to God. Prayer is simply you and God talking. God searches the heart, so just make sure your prayer is authentic.

And don't feel like God can't handle your prayers. He can.

So when Nehemiah began to rebuild, they hated him. When he continued to build, they hated him more. So what do you need to do when the threat from the enemy becomes even stronger?

Respond with a Guard

As Nehemiah and his team continued to rebuild, the Bible says, "They [the enemies] all plotted together to come and fight against Jerusalem and stir up trouble against it" (Neh. 4:8). You are probably asking yourself, "Does it get any easier?" The answer is no. The more you move forward, the more the enemy is going to turn his heat up. But I have good news! You have more power than the enemy. You have the source, God, on your side. Don't be surprised when more hell breaks loose in your life. At this point some gaps were being closed in the wall so when you begin to close some of the gaps (hurt, pain, shame) in your life, expect more opposition.

Nehemiah responded in a different way this time. The Bible says he prayed and posted a guard twenty-four hours to meet the threat.

With this in mind, you need to enlist some people who can cover you in prayer. These prayer warriors are going to be your guards. Tell them to not let up until your rebuilding process is done. The apostle Paul was facing imprisonment but he trusted that God was going to deliver and protect him. Paul said, "For I know that through *your prayers* and God's provision of the Spirit of Jesus Christ what has happened to me will turn out for my deliverance" (Phil. 1:19, emphasis mine).

If you noticed in the scripture, Paul acknowledged the fact that the prayers of the saints will help in his deliverance. One can put a thousand to flight but two can put ten thousand to flight (Deut. 32:30).

Peter was locked in prison for preaching the gospel as well. Because prayers were made without ceasing to God, Peter's chains fell off his hands. The iron gate opened and he was led out of the prison by an angel of God (Acts 12:5–12). This shows the power of having some people cover you in prayer!

Respond by Helping Others

As Nehemiah was facing his opposition, he stopped and helped the poor (Neh. 5:1–19). It does not make sense from the outside to help someone else while you are trying to rebuild but if you really think about, it makes all the sense in the world. Not only will you be rebuilding but helping someone else rebuild at the same time. What a great way to give the devil two black eyes! Remember: one rebuilding story can put one thousand to flight. Two rebuilding stories can put ten thousand to flight.

I enjoy going out and speaking and sharing my story. But I really enjoy hearing the testimonials of how people find hope and encouragement from what I have endured. It gives them the willpower to keep pushing forward. Not only do I want to rebuild but I also want to see others rebuild with me. See, I'm trying to give the devil a heart attack. I can't react to what has been done or taken from me but I can respond by helping others find purpose and hope.

Think about who you can help. If you have filed bankruptcy, you can help share the importance of budgeting. If you are rebounding from cancer, you can go back to the cancer center and tell the new patients that they can rebuild. Do you see the big picture? Reacting to a setback and not sharing your experience can hinder someone from rebuilding. But responding with a helpful heart can help set someone free.

Respond with the Same

If you are a parent, you can fully understand my pain concerning snack time and then the time after snack time. Snack time never ends as long as you have something in the cabinet. It is much easier when you stick to the no. My children actually leave me alone after several no's. Try it. It actually works if you stay consistent.

Nehemiah responded the same way to his opposition. When the wall was almost built, the enemy plotted to harm Nehemiah. The enemy sent Nehemiah a letter to meet them twenty miles from where he was rebuilding the wall so they could ambush him. Don't be surprised if the enemy tries to do the same to you. Don't let him lure you into a trap. Let's look and see how Nehemiah responded:

Opposition: Sanballat and Geshem sent me this message: "Come, let us meet together in one of the villages on the plain of Ono."
Response: But they were scheming to harm me; so I sent messengers to them with this reply: "I am carrying on a great project and cannot go down. Why should the work stop while I leave it and go down to you?" (Neh. 6:2–3)

Nehemiah said, "Four times they sent me the same message, and each time I gave them the same answer" (Neh. 6:4). There is power in the same. Whatever you are endeavoring to rebuild, you have incorporate the word *no* into your vocabulary. The enemy is going to do all he can to stop you as you get closer to your goal of finishing.

Saying no does not come easy to a lot of people, especially me. But I have learned that when I have a goal I am trying to reach, no is not a bad word to tell the enemy.

My mornings would go something like this:

Curtis, give up on your dreams. Nope.

Curtis, you are wasting your time. Nope.

Curtis, try something else. Nope.

It doesn't matter how much opposition the enemy brings into your life, you give him the same answer: you are not going to quit.

Respond by Staying in the Race

In the 2012 Olympics people were watching Usain Bolt but something else happened that was even bigger: Manteo Mitchell running the four hundred meters with a broken leg. What was so amazing about his race is that his fibula broke midway through the race. That means he had to finish the race on a broken leg. How is that possible? I believe he said to himself that he was going to stay in the race, regardless of the broken leg. He could not stop because his team was relying on him to finish. Nehemiah had that same determination to finish, even though he was facing his greatest opposition.

The enemy sent word to Nehemiah and asked him to meet him in the house of God. Shemiah did not want to meet Nehemiah in the house of God to pray with him but to get him in there so he could trick Nehemiah so the enemy could harm him. Nehemiah refused the invitation. Nehemiah said, "Should a man like me run away? Or should one like me go into the temple to save his life? I will not go!" (Neh. 6:11)

You are probably wondering where Nehemiah found so much strength. A few verses earlier, Nehemiah asked God to strengthen his hands. (Neh. 6:9)

Nehemiah did not ask God to take him out of the situation, although the enemy was threatening his life. Likewise, I want you to respond by asking God to strengthen your hands when you feel like giving up. Ask for strength to stay in the race, not to get you out the race.

I was at a breaking point four years ago. I am not going to lie; it was the lowest I have ever been in my life. When the doctors told my family that my brother would never live a normal life again because he had lost too much oxygen to the brain, I crumbled. Around the same time, I found out that my son was missing chromosome number 16, which causes developmental delays and some other things. These two bad reports at the same time crippled my faith. I just remember getting on my knees and asking God to give me strength because I wanted to give up. David said, "In my distress I called to the LORD; I cried to my God for help. From his temple he heard my voice; my cry came before him, into his ears" (Ps. 18:6). If you cry out to God for strength, he will listen. God gives strength to the weak (Isa. 40:20).

You have a prize that you are running toward so stay in the race until you reach the finish line. The opposition that you will encounter cannot compare to the prize that is in store for you.

If you quit, you will never get to see the new you. It will get better over time. When opposition comes, remember to respond with the source, with prayer, with a guard (prayer warrior), with the same answer, and by staying in the race.

THINGS TO REMEMBER

1. Opposition is going to happen, especially when you are trying to rebuild. The key is to not react but respond. Remember to respond and keep moving forward with the process.

2. Don't be surprised if the level of opposition increases as you grow. The closer you get to the finish line, the more you will have to fight to stay in the race. The level of your opposition is an indication of the level of breakthroughs ahead.

If you find a *why* to get up for, then meeting your goals will not be an issue.

—Curtis Rice

Step 6

Identify Your Why

Identifying your why is one of the most important steps you will need to take as you move forward in life. You have the vision and plans but the why will help you get up when you don't feel like it. Friedrich Nietzsche, a German philosopher of the late nineteenth century, asserted, "He who has a why to live for can bear almost any how." You have to find a *why* to live and to rebuild for. When you find it, you'll find the energy to walk through any storm that may occur.

I visited my younger brother in the nursing home for four years before his death. It hurts me to even write this chapter because his death is recent but I have the strength to write because he is the why for this book. I am determined to make it to the next stage in my life because of him. I can't quit because I would be quitting on him. He has three beautiful girls that I would love to help send to college and do many more things for in the future, so I work extra hard to make sure I will be able to.

When my grandpa would go out and slave in the hot sun, his why was to provide for his family. Nehemiah had a why as well, his kinfolk to be protected by the wall.

What is your *why*? If you do not find a *why*, it is going to be hard to rebuild. I am going to give you some reasons why the *why* is so important. This is how the *why* has helped me throughout the years.

It Will Help You Stay Motivated

After my father passed away when I was seventeen, it motivated me to become a good father, husband, and leader. For instance, because I did not get to spend a lot of time with my father, it created an urgency in me to spend quality time with my children. I have turned the pain of his death into motivation. I have a goal one day to do something in his name, like starting the LG leadership academy. With that goal in mind, I am motivated to learn all I can about leadership so I can make that dream a reality.

I don't like to read all the time. I don't like to research for hours and hours. I don't like to sit at home in front of my computer and pursue my doctorate degree in organizational leadership. But I am motivated to see LG leadership academy in action, which will build strong leaders for tomorrow.

Every morning I get up and I say to myself, *LG leadership academy is changing lives, building dreams, and raising up strong leaders.* Do you see how I have turned his death into motivation? I can't stop. When I see him again in heaven, I want to be able to tell him about the leadership academy that I built in his name.

It Will Help You Stay Focused

When you are trying to rebuild, you must put your life into laser focus mode and the why will help.

My father and I did not have a good relationship but it did get better as time went on. I will never forget the two things he asked me the morning of his death. He said, "Do you want some breakfast?" I said, "No, Dad." Then he said, "Are you going to graduate?" I said, "Yes, Dad." Unfortunately, I did not graduate high school. I dropped out in the last semester of my senior year after his death.

Because I did not get to graduate high school and he did not get to see me receive my adult high school diploma, it created a hunger in me to attain the highest educational level possible: a doctoral degree.

Since I started the journey, I have encountered many setbacks and obstacles, like the death of my grandpa while I was pursuing my undergrad degree. The accident of my brother happened when I was pursuing my undergrad as well.

Even though some people felt sorry for me and told me that I had an excuse to quit, I could not let my father down. I promised him that I was going to graduate. I came across a quote on focus by an unknown author that said, "If you chase two rabbits, both will escape."

When you find your *why* it will help you stay focused on one rabbit. You are going to have a lot of things that desire your attention. Don't lose focus and chase after two rabbits. Both will escape and then you are left with nothing at the end of the day. My father (my *why*) is helping me stay focused on finishing my doctoral dissertation.

It Will Help You Stay Grateful

I sat down to eat dinner with my family after leaving the nursing home one super-hot evening. I stopped eating, with spaghetti sauce sliding down my face, and looked up at my wife and told her that I was grateful for being able to eat and walk. It is the little things in life that we forget to be thankful and grateful about.

Because of the accident my brother lost the ability to eat and walk. It hurt me to see him go through that but it made me grateful for the ability to eat and walk. You are probably wondering what does being grateful have to do with rebuilding? It has everything to do with rebuilding. You need to be grateful for every step you make toward your goal. Do not take it for granted. There are millions of people who would love to trade positions with you right now. They would love to be able to walk in your footsteps for one day, some for even one hour.

When I wake up in the morning now, I am grateful for another day to pursue my goals and dreams. My brother does not have the privilege to go after his dreams. I am grateful to be able to play with my kids. My brother does not have the privilege to play with his girls. Since I am grateful, I do not waste time doing things that are not productive, which has helped me move forward in life.

It Will Help You Eliminate Excuses

The crazy thing about my brother being in the nursing home is that he did not let that take his smile away. The same smile he had before the accident he had in the nursing home. Even though he could not eat normally like you and me and could not talk normally like you and me and could not walk like you and me, he still smiled.

I walked away from the nursing home, after looking at him smile from ear to ear, and said to myself, *I have no more excuses. I have no more excuses. There is nothing or no one that can stop me from living out my dreams.*

Yes, some bad things did happen in your life. But you have to move from the victim mentality to the victor mentality. It is going to be hard to rebuild if you are still living on Excuse Street. Pack your clothes and move to No More Excuses Avenue.

Nick Vujicic, one of the greatest motivational speakers in the world, was born with no limbs. He is conquering the world and changing lives with no limbs. My Aunt, Melissa, who I mentioned in the dedication, battled stage 4 cancer with a smile on her face. When I think about my brother, Melissa, and Nick, I say to myself, "I have no excuse for not living up to my fullest potential."

The only thing standing between you and your goal of rebuilding a better you is an excuse about why you can't. Don't allow it to hinder you from seeing who you are created to be. Florence Nightingale, an English nurse, writer and statistician, once said, "I attribute my success to this—I never gave or took any excuse."

The moment I moved beyond making excuses, was the moment I gradually witnessed my life change for the better. Your father may have walked out on you. Your husband may have left. You may have lost your job. Dust yourself off. Gather your thoughts. Tell that excuse that you are no longer going to let it take another day from your life. You are going to rebuild. You are not going to give or make an excuse.

It Will Help You Have a Change in Perspective

I hit a lot of very low moments seeing my brother in the nursing home. In those moments, I tried to go and listen to other preachers or turn on something positive on YouTube. This particular moment I decided to take a long Saturday evening drive and go to church, just to receive a Word from God. Let me take a detour and say that God is still speaking. At times, we let our circumstances drown out the voice of God. Sometimes we get so blinded by what's taken from us that we forget about what God is doing through us. Another message for another time. But let me continue with the book.

As I sat down in the chair the usher escorted me to, thoughts of throwing all of my dreams I had in the trash were flowing through my head—and just doing something to take care of my family until I get old, and go home to be with the Lord when I die. That was my thought process at the time.

The preacher picked up some binoculars and said that we look at our situations through the wrong lens. When you look through the binoculars the way they were intended to be used, the object appears to be bigger than you. But when you flip them around, your situation looks smaller. God looks at our situations through this side of the lens, he continued.

One main reason people make excuses is because they have the wrong perspective about their situation. Sometimes our situation is not as big as it seems. And if it is bad, it is not bad enough for God. He can handle what we are going through.

From that Saturday forward, I started looking at my situation through the eyes of God. Did the situation immediately change because I had a change in perspective? No. But it helped me find faith and hope in tragedy. It also helped me with a lot of stress, stress that was hurting my health.

Try it. It is pretty cool. Go to Wal-Mart and buy some binoculars. And when another situation occurs while you are rebuilding a better you, turn the binoculars around and say to the opposition, "You are nothing. You are small compared to the big God I serve." The enemy strives to make a situation look worse than what it is. Let's have a change in perspective.

THINGS TO REMEMBER

1. Find a *why* to get up for, to rebuild for. If you do not have a *why*, it is going to be hard to rebuild. The *why* will give encouragement to keep rebuilding when you don't feel like it. The *why* will give you the courage to fight any battle.

2. Create a list of why's that explains why you do what you do. Here are some of my why's:

   My wife is the reason why I get up and have a deep desire to be all I can be.
   My children are the reasons why I want to leave a legacy and inheritance.
   My brother is the reason why I smile and make no excuses.
   My father is the reason why I work so hard to become a better leader.
   Jesus is the reason why I preach the kingdom of God.

   When you find a *why* for what you do, you will have no problem with rebuilding.

Just imagine what would have happened if Michael Jordan quit after getting cut from his high school basketball team?

—John Passaro

Step 7

Don't Stop

You have made it to the last step in the book and I have saved the best for last. It is time to make a decision that you are not going to stop. When people hear my story, they are amazed that I am still standing. Studies say that people who have been through what I have been through should be in prison, on drugs, depressed, and a long list of other bad things. But I have made a subconscious decision that I am not going to stop. I am going to continue to grow, think, and learn. I want you to tell yourself that you are not going to give up, no matter what occurs in your life.

Nehemiah made a decision before he started rebuilding the walls that he was not going to stop. The Bible doesn't say that he literally said "I am not going stop" but you can see it in his actions as he faced much opposition.

I am not a scholar. I am not the smartest person in the world. But quitting is not in my blood. Life is full of pain. You cannot run from it, nor can you hide from it. You will have to face it. What would your life look like in five years if you don't stop pursuing that degree? What would your life look like in five years if you decide to eat healthy? What would your life look like if you pursue your dreams like never before? What would your life look like if you decide to be the best you? Why wonder? You can do it—just decide to not stop. It is going to take everything in you to not stop. That is a promise but I would like to share some things with you that helped me.

Find Courage

After Moses had passed away, God chose a new leader by the name of Joshua to lead the children of Israel to the Promised Land. This was not an easy task. Moses was a great leader. He led the first mega church of two million plus! However, God told Joshua to take courage for he would be with him (Joshua 1:9). Edward Cummings, a poem writer in the early 1900s, said that "It takes courage to grow up and become who you really are." I want you to become the new you, the person you really are, but it is going to take courage.

Joshua had the gift in him to be an amazing leader, just like Moses, but at the beginning of his early leadership journey, he needed someone to tell him to take courage. I want you to find courage. Brian Tracy says, "The way to develop the courage you need is to act as if you already had the courage and behave accordingly."

This is a good way to find courage: to act like you already have it. Say to yourself that you are smart enough to go back to school and go after that degree. Walk into class every day with your head up. Say to yourself that you can be a good husband, no matter what they have said about you and no matter how your father treated you. Go home after work with your head up. Say to yourself that you can get that job. Go into the interview like the job is already yours.

When I started pursuing my master's degree, I did not have the courage. The enemy constantly told me over and over that I was a high school dropout and no way could I get a master's degree. But I signed up and acted like I did have the courage and behaved accordingly. After each class, my courage grew stronger and stronger. Before I knew it, I was walking across the finish line with my diploma. No matter how many papers I was asked to write, I said to myself that I could do it. *I am a great writer. I can read. I can do the research.* I want you to find that same courage.

Mistakes Will Happen

I was in charge of leading Youth Sunday. When the fifth Sunday came, the childcare teacher told me to call the kids up at the end of service because she had been working with them on a surprise for their parents. I was super pumped about the lineup. It was a great one! Everything flowed so well. So I thought.

At the end of the service, the childcare teacher walked up to me and said, "Curtis, you forgot to call us forward." When she said those six words to me, they flowed through my body in slow motion like the matrix. Most horrible of all, she had prepared and the kids were anticipating this moment to shine.

I went home that day and curled up in my bed and wished that I could stay there forever. It is unfortunate that I had to learn the importance not only of having a good outline but of asking for more help from that experience. Although I still regret that Sunday from the bottom of my heart, I learned so much from that mistake, but even more importantly, I learned that mistakes are going to happen. The key is to learn how to rebound from them.

Let me free you from some stress. You are going to make mistakes as you move forward. The Bible says that a just (righteous) man falls down seven times but he gets back up (Prov. 24:16). God is already aware that we are going to make mistakes. Mistakes do not catch him by surprise.

However, God is not okay with you to staying down after you make one. Don't let the mistakes of your past keep you in the bed for hours but instead use them as fuel to make it to the next level. I have a saying that I use now, "Marry mistakes, divorce success."

Mistakes are actually good to make. They help you grow and learn, but only if you evaluate them afterwards. The day after I made that mistake, I called the childcare teacher and apologized. Then I sat down in my thinking chair and thought about how I could not make the same mistake again. That one experience, after evaluation, has helped me grow as a leader, father, and husband.

So if you make a mistake, don't be so hard on yourself. Ralph Nadar asserts, "Your best teacher is your last mistake." So don't stop moving forward when you make one. There are four things I want you to do when you make a mistake: Sit. Think. Evaluate. Implement.

Sit. I want you to stop what you are doing and sit. I have a chair that I like to sit in. Find a special spot in your house. Sometimes I get up early or I do it before I go to bed. I want you to make it a ritual. Trust me, it will help you rebuild much faster.

Think. The next thing I want you to do is think about the mistake. Think through the whole process in your mind, step by step. This will program it in your mind so the next time a similar situation comes up; your mind will immediately go into protection mode or "Let's not do that again" mode.

Evaluate. Now it is time to evaluate the situation. Determine how bad the situation is. Sometimes our mistakes are minor but we make them out to be something major. If the mistake falls into the minor (did not have a direct effect on others) category, keep moving forward.

Often I make minor mistakes trying to put things together. These things, such as a book shelf, have no effect on others, just on myself and my books. This is a minor mistake.

If it falls into the major category (has a direct effect on others), figure out how you could have done it better. This will program your mind to store the solution into your memory bank. The mistake I made on Youth Sunday is a major mistake.

Implement. It does no good if you are not going to make what you have learned a part of your life. From the Youth Sunday experience, I have learned to ask for help. I was too busy that Sunday trying to make sure the program had no gaps. I should have found someone to help me with the service. Now, I try to ask for help.

Live for the Moment

Tomorrow is yet to be born. Yesterday is dead. Today (the moment) is alive. Today is all we have. It is alive and breathing. If you focus on the moment, it will help you not quit. In fact, today's activities will build your tomorrow, not your past. Trust me, tomorrow will work itself out when you live for the moment.

Don't get stuck in the past. It is gone so leave it there. If you have done something horrible, let it go. Rebuild in this present moment.

This principle has helped me so much. Think about it: there is nothing like the moment. We can build a new tomorrow by what we do today!

Start improving your attitude today. Start writing the book you have been wishing to write today. Start working on that degree today. Start improving your marriage, today. Before you know it, in two or three weeks you'll see a big change, if you get up every day and work on it.

Anytime I work on a new project, I focus on what I can do today. I take a look at the end picture and then break it down into steps that I can take every day. This has helped me to not stop on so many projects, especially big ones.

When I focused on yesterday, today, and tomorrow, I got nothing done. John Maxwell observed, "People create success in their lives by focusing on today. It may sound trite, but today is the only time you have." Today is all you have so I want you to put your total focus on it. Tell your past goodbye, tell today you are here, and tell tomorrow that you will see it soon!

Celebrate Today

When I turned twenty-one, it was one of the best days of my life. My pastor called me and asked me to go with him to Cracker Barrel, one of my favorite restaurants. You know I could not turn down a good old apple deep dish apple pie with a little ice cream on top. I always tell my waitress to make sure they heat it up my pie so the vanilla ice cream can melt down into my pie. I hope you are not reading this book to rebuild your health; if so, sorry but that pie is delicious!

On the way there, my pastor told me that he had to stop by a church member's house. So we did. I was a little upset because for one, it was my birthday. Second, it was my birthday. Who wants to spend their birthday stopping by houses? I quietly got out the car and walked to the front door with him.

You are probably wondering what happened next. Nothing. Just kidding.

The door slowly cracked opened. With my head looking down to the ground, I put one foot in the house, wondering why I was there on my birthday. Then all of a sudden, I heard the most beautiful harmony in my life sing, "Happy Birthday!"

Wow. I will never forget that moment in my life. I had my first birthday party at the age of twenty-one.

When I was young, I did not know how to celebrate. We never celebrated anything. So it rolled over into my young adulthood. But that special day taught me that it is okay to celebrate, especially when you have accomplished something.

Rebuilding your life is something to celebrate. I want you to celebrate every day at the end of the day. Have yourself a party. If you are setting a goal to quit smoking, celebrate every day you go without one. If you are setting a goal to quit drinking, celebrate every day you go without one.

I take the time to celebrate every day I write. I give myself a gift to look forward to at the end of the day. Before I know it, my goal of finishing another book is one day closer. Now, you can't celebrate too long because tomorrow you have to start all over again. A new day demands a new celebration, not a new day with an old celebration. Remember, today's success means nothing tomorrow.

Celebrating small victories will not only help you not stop but give you the courage to tackle the bigger things you will face tomorrow.

In the Old Testament, the children of Israel were afraid of a giant by the name of Goliath. I mean he was pretty big. No one would fight him but a small-framed boy by the name of David. David had the courage to fight Goliath because he had killed a lion and a bear. David said, "Your servant has killed both the lion and the bear; this uncircumcised Philistine will be like one of them, because he has defied the armies of the living God" (1 Sam. 17:36). The past victories gave David the courage to fight today's problem (Goliath). Celebrate today!

Keep the Right Attitude

Keeping the right attitude is a must. It is not an option. Attitude is the difference maker as, Dr. John Maxwell would say. Winston Churchill rightfully observed, "Attitude is a little thing that makes a big difference." I remember sitting at the hospital with my brother for almost forty-five days and him not responding to anything. From the reality of the circumstance, I had a decision to make: I could have a negative attitude or I could have a positive attitude. I decided to have a positive attitude.

I would go to the hospital and say to myself that my brother would respond again. He was going to know who his family was. He was going to know his children. It was not easy because the current circumstances looked like he wouldn't.

After being in the hospital for almost two months, my family had a choice to put him in Hospice Care or send him to a nursing home, believing that he was going to respond again. We chose to put him in a nursing home. My nursing visits would go something like this:

Boo Boo, can you hear me? It's okay, my friend. See you tomorrow.

Boo Boo, can you hear me? It's okay. Maybe not this time. See you tomorrow.

Boo Boo, can you hear me? It's okay. Maybe you are too tired. See you tomorrow.

Boo Boo, can you hear me? It's okay. I'm not going to give up. See you tomorrow.

Boo Boo, can you hear me? It's okay, buddy. I'll just read this book to you. See you on tomorrow.

As I was visiting him, the nurse asked me if I wanted to take him outside. I said sure. She and some other nurses pulled him off of his bed and placed him inside the wheelchair.

I pushed him outside and sat with him as the sun was scorching down on our faces. I pulled up a chair beside him and said, "Boo Boo, can you hear me?"

Wait a minute; I believe he is trying to talk. I believe I saw his lips move. I said, "Boo Boo." His lips slowly opened and uttered, "What?" And then a tear drop rolled down his face, as one rolled down mine.

That day proved to me what can happen when you don't stop and keep the right attitude. I watched a miracle happen that day.

Talk to Yourself

What? You are probably thinking, *Is this guy crazy?* But that is exactly what I want you to do: talk to yourself. Solomon, one of the wisest men to ever live, said, "The tongue has the power of life and death, and those who love it will eat its fruit" (Prov. 18:21). Words have power, so that is why I want you to talk to yourself. Keep saying to yourself that you are going to make it. No matter how bad it looks, you are going to make it. Tell that voice in your mind that you are going to win!

There were days when I did not feel like being positive. There were days when I just wanted to close all the blinds and lock myself in the house. But what helped me was the ability to tell myself that I was going to make it. I would outlast this storm. I would outlast this pain.

When you talk to yourself, you are actually programming your mind. Then your body will follow what your mind says. So if you talk negative, then negative words will be programmed in your mind. The body, in turn, will feel sick and depressed.

Think about if you used positive words instead of negative ones.

You are your biggest cheerleader so you need to learn how to encourage yourself. When all else fails and no one is there to support you on your journey of rebuilding a better you, you can talk to yourself.

Tell yourself that you are going to make it.

Tell yourself that you have greatness in you.

Tell yourself that you have a purpose.

Tell yourself that you are not a mistake.

Tell yourself that you will outlast this storm.

Tell yourself that you are more than a conqueror.

Tell yourself that you are smart.

Tell yourself that you are going to act accordingly.

See, you can feel a difference already. When you talk positive to yourself, you are giving life to your dream. When you talk negative to yourself, you are suffocating your dream. Your dream needs life.

I want you to try it for twenty-one days and see if you do not see a difference in your life. I tell myself all the time, *Curtis, just take one more step*.

When I was in high school, I worked for an organization called WIA, which allowed teenagers to work over the summer. One summer they had a guest speaker to come in. This tall man with a gentle spirit walked in and scared the living day lights out of all of us, especially me. I mean I was 5' 9" weighing about 140lbs, and he was like 6' 4", looking like a giant. I will never forget what he said to me. I guess he saw that I was lost, with no future. He looked me in the eye and said, "You are somebody." I glanced over to another student because I knew he wasn't talking to me. He walked a little closer to me, looking at me with razor sharp eyes, and said, "You are somebody."

Looking eye to eye, he said, "Repeat after me: I am somebody." I said, "I am somebody." I will never forget that moment. It was the turning point for me. When I get down, I look at myself in the mirror and say, "I am somebody." When I want to give up, I look at myself in the mirror and say, "I am somebody." I am where I am today because I believe that I am somebody. The motivational speaker I was talking about is now my good friend and one of my mentors. Because of him, I tell myself over and over again that I am somebody.

Find an Outlet

Trying to rebuild your life is going to get frustrating at times. Therefore, you are going to need an outlet. This will help you cool down and get back in the game of rebuilding. There are many outlets you can have, such as running or watching a good movie.

When I need to find peace, I usually turn on some worship music or listen to nature sounds. Now, you do not need to do the same things I do but you do need to find an outlet. If you get frustrated, go find a punching bag. Some people like to go to an open field and scream at the top of their lungs. I have a friend who likes to go to a driving range to let out frustrations.

Jesus Christ had an outlet. He would go to a quiet place and pray to his father.

I have a good friend that I call and ask him to give me five minutes to vent all of my anger and then give me some advice. This has helped me tremendously. If you do not find an outlet, all of the anger will build up inside and then you'll explode and wonder how in the world you got there. I have been there. It is not a good feeling. You will end up hurting someone you deeply care about.

Creating an outlet has helped me to not stop several times. Before I started writing this book, I was working on another one. The flash drive became damaged and six months of writing was gone. An outlet helped me to sit back down and start on a new one called *Rebuild*. Look at the outlet as a place to bury your frustrations of today so you can deal with the new frustrations that tomorrow will bring.

Ask Questions

Ask yourself what will happen if you stop. Ask yourself how your life would change if you make it to the finish line. How many more people will you be able to help? What skills do you need to upgrade to make it to the next level?

Don't be afraid to ask questions. If you are not asking questions, you are not learning. I ask questions all the time now. You are going to need to find new answers to make it from one season to the next season in your life. Asking questions is the way to find out.

Don't give up if you hit a ceiling or a brick wall. Someone has already been through what you are currently facing, and they can give you free wisdom!

I had a Honda Accord that I could not figure out why the battery was going dead and not warming up. I had to go outside early in the morning, around 4:30, to jump the car off. I did this for an entire winter. Honestly, I wanted to give up on the car. I believe I started looking for another car as I think about it.

After church, I asked a mechanic for some advice. He came over to the car and found the problem in less than one minute, and fixed the issue in less than two minutes.

I could have saved some cold, cold mornings. All I had to do was ask. Don't be like me. This car turned out to be one of the best cars I have ever owned. Before you decide to quit, ask questions. The answer for you not quitting may be found in less than two minutes!

Find a Mentor

As you are rebuilding, find a mentor, someone you can look up to for guidance and direction. If you cannot find a mentor, books are a great resource. I have several mentors. Some are distant. Some are close. The mentors I cannot come in direct contact with, I consider my distant mentors. I learn from them through the books they have written and I attend their seminars. The mentors I can contact, I call my close mentors.

I've wanted to give up several times but my mentors have been there to help me. Please find some mentors. I am not talking about your friends on Facebook. Find some mentors that can help you. Find some mentors that have made a mark on earth. Find mentors that can call out that potential inside you. One of my close mentors told me that I had more potential than him. It shocked me because he travels the world speaking. Paulo Coelho observed, "What is a teacher? I'll tell you: it isn't someone who teaches something, but someone who inspires the student to give of her best in order to discover what she already knows." You need mentors that can inspire and help you find what is already in you.

Get Fired Up

It is time to get fired up. You are about to change your life. You will never be the same. You are about to give birth to a new you. I know it to be true. The steps in the book can change your life if you use them.

If you have made it this far in the book, it means that you have a hunger to change your life. I believe God is going to honor that hunger and help you rebuild.

I heard a preacher say to a class of soon-to-be preachers that you do not have to beg people to come to your church. You do not have to bribe them to come either. The preacher told them to forget about all of that. He said the only thing you have to do is catch on fire and people will travel from long distances to come watch you burn.

You don't have to wish for a better life anymore. You don't have to beg for a better life anymore. Just work through the steps found in this book and success will come find you. In other words, grow you—and everything else will have to grow.

No longer will you be bound to your past. No longer will you say to yourself that you cannot do it. No longer will you second-guess whether you were created for a purpose. No longer will you live like there is no hope. No longer will you make an excuse.

It is time to get fired up because you are taking the best journey of your life, the road to rebuilding a better you.

Nehemiah practiced all seven steps found in this book. He laid a strong foundation. He had a vision. He drafted a few. He examined. He expected opposition. He had a *why*. And he did not quit. Because of these steps, and with God's help, the wall was completed in fifty-two days. (Neh. 6:15)

THINGS TO REMEMBER

1. Resolve in your mind that you are not going to quit, no matter how hard it gets. Tell yourself that quitting is not an option. Don't be afraid to ask questions if you hit a brick wall.

2. When you take a positive step, take time to celebrate. Reward yourself with a treat. Don't take today's celebration into tomorrow. A new day, requires a new celebration.

Conclusion

What to Do from This Day Forward

The book has given you some great steps to rebuild your life. I have not written something that is false. These principles have helped me enjoy life and regain a sense of purpose and hope. They have helped me overcome depression. They have helped me meet goals and do things I couldn't even imagine doing.

From this day forward, I want you to keep this book near you. The steps found in the book can work at any point in your life. Rebuilding is an ongoing process. You will never stop rebuilding, unless you choose to do so. Make a commitment that you are going to see the new you.

I want to challenge you to work these steps into your daily life. When you wake up in the morning, lay a foundation. See a vision for your life. Draft a few people to support you. Examine yourself. Expect opposition. Identify your *why* and don't stop. If you do these things, you will rebuild. It is just a matter of time. Nothing and no one can stop you but yourself.

Let's rebuild!

Notes

Chapter 1—Lay the Foundation

1. Nehemiah 1:11
2. Nehemiah 1:2
3. Nehemiah 1:3
4. Nehemiah 1:4
5. Brian Tracy, *No Excuses: The Power of Self-Discipline* (New York, NY: MTF Books, 2010), 5.
6. Luke 5:37
7. Joyce Meyer, *You Can Begin Again* (New York, NY: Hachette, 2014, p. 24.)
8. Nehemiah 2:2
9. Mark 9:29
10. James 2:14–26
11. Quote retrieved from http://www.goodreads.com/quotes/53121-self-discipline-is-the-ability-to-make-yourself-do-what-you

Chapter 2—See the Vision

1. Quote retrieved from http://www.brainyquote.com/quotes/quotes/r/rosabethmo390507.html
2. Quote retrieved from http://www.movemequotes.com/top-10-steve-jobs-quotes/

3. Steve Harvey, *Act Like a Success Think Like a Success* (New York, NY: HarperCollins, 2014), 129.
4. Genesis 12:2–3
5. Genesis 15:5
6. T. D. Jakes, *Instinct: The Power to Unleash Your Inborn Drive* (New York, NY: Hachette, 2014), 45.
7. Retrieved from http://www.accademia.org/explore-museum/artworks/michelangelos-david/
8. Nehemiah 2:12
9. Matthew 16:23
10. Habakkuk 2:2

Chapter 3—Draft a Few

1. See 1 Kings 19:19
2. Luke 6:12

Chapter 4—Examination

1. Nehemiah 2:13–15
2. Quote retrieved from http://www.goodreads.com/quotes/tag/exams
3. Quote retrieved from http://www.brainyquote.com/quotes/quotes/d/dwightdei149111.html
4. Nehemiah 2:6
5. See Judges 7:7
6. Retrieved from http://mashable.com/2016/06/18/revel-systems-lisa-falzone/#LN8aYc6TAqqg
7. Retrieved from http://www.investopedia.com/terms/p/pareto principle.asp
8. Quote retrieved from http://www.goodreads.com/quotes/432412-i-insist-on-a-lot-of-time-being-spent-almost
9. Nehemiah 3:16
10. Nehemiah 2:17–18

11. Nehemiah 2:20
12. Nehemiah 4:1
13. Nehemiah 4:4–5
14. Exodus 14:14
15. 2 Chronicles 20;17
16. Philippians 1:6
17. Nehemiah 4:18
18. Acts 12:5–12
19. See Nehemiah 5:1–19
20. Philippians 1:19
21. Nehemiah 6:2–3
22. Nehemiah 6:4
23. Nehemiah 6:11
24. Nehemiah 6:9
25. Psalm 18:6
26. Isaiah 40:20

Chapter 5—Expect Opposition

1. Nehemiah 2:17–18
2. Nehemiah 2:20
3. Luke 20:43
4. Romans 8:31
5. Joel Osteen, *It's Your Time* (New York, NY: Free Press, 2009), 150.
6. Exodus 14:14
7. Acts 12:5–12
8. See Nehemiah 5:1–19
9. Isaiah 40:20

Chapter 6—Identify Your Why

1. Quote retrieved from http://www.goodreads.com/quotes/137-he-who-has-a-why-to-live-for-can-bear

2. Quote retrieved from http://www.brainyquote.com/quotes/quotes/f/florenceni391864.html

Chapter 7—Don't Stop

1. Joshua 1:9
2. Quote retrieved from http://www.brainyquote.com/quotes/quotes/e/eecummin161593.html
3. Bryan Tracy, *Eat That Frog* (San Francisco, CA: Berrett-Koehler, 2007), 59.
4. Proverbs 24:16
5. Quote retrieved from http://www.brainyquote.com/quotes/quotes/r/ralphnader100299.html
6. John Maxwell, *Today Matters* (New York, NY: Hachette, 2004), 10.
7. Quote retrieved from http://www.brainyquote.com/quotes/quotes/w/winstonchu104164.html
8. 1 Samuel 17:36
9. Proverbs 18:21
10. Quote retrieved from http://www.goodreads.com/quotes/37661-what-is-a-teacher-i-ll-tell-you-it-isn-t-someone
11. Nehemiah 6:15

Index

F

faith, 9, 37, 54, 61
Falzone, Lisa, 40
family, 7–9, 18, 21, 30, 54, 57, 59, 61, 71
fasting, 7, 9
finances, 21, 38
foundation, 1, 3, 5, 9–11, 22, 31, 35, 43, 81
strong, 3, 10–11, 77
Fox News, ix

G

Genesis, 16
Gideon (Israelite leader), 39
gifts, 16, 38, 66, 70
God, 5, 7–9, 16–21, 23, 25, 33, 38–39, 47–51, 53–54, 61, 66–67, 76–77
Goliath (Philistine giant), 71
grieving, 4–5
guard, 50–51, 54

H

habit replacement, 42
habits, 39–43, 45
bad, 41, 43
new, 41–42, 45
Harvey, Steve, 16
heart, 9–11, 19–20, 25, 50, 52, 67
hunger, 58, 76

I

imagination, 16
Israel, 38, 66, 71

J

Jakes, T. D., 18
Jerusalem, xii, 2, 9, 17, 19–20, 22, 25, 27–28, 35–38, 47, 50
Jesus, 3, 9, 20, 22, 26, 49, 51, 74
Jews, 2, 7, 43, 50
Joseph (Hebrew patriarch), 18
Joshua (Israelite leader), 66
journey, 22, 25, 29, 31, 37–38, 59

K

Kanter, Rosabeth, 15

L

ladder, 27–30, 33
leader, 1, 18, 41, 58, 63, 66–67
strong, 58
leadership, 17, 38, 41, 58, 66
LG leadership academy, 58

M

marriage, 4, 9, 15, 36–37, 42, 69
Maxwell, John, 41–42, 69, 71
mentors, 75–76
Michelangelo, 18–19
miracle, xii, 9, 38, 72
mistakes, 67–68, 73
Moses (Hebrew prophet), 38, 66

Printed in the United States
By Bookmasters